Nate & Shea's
Adventures in
PERU

By Carrie Whitten-Simmons
with help and journal entries from
Nathan and Seamus, hosts of the
television series
Travel With Kids

Dedicated to Eli - Thanks for sharing your knowledge and showing us
your amazing country. Your enthusiasm is contagious!
And thanks to all the families who joined us on this trip!

Haykuykuy! That means welcome in Quechua, a language of the Incan Empire. With clashes between different tribes, and the Incans and the Spanish conquistadors, Peru's history sparks the imagination. Plus, the Amazon Rainforest is home to 40,000 plant species and almost 5,000 kinds of animals not including the 2 1/2 million kinds of insects! Join us, Nate and Shea, hosts of television series *Travel With Kids*, as we discover the history, culture and nature of Peru and stop for lots of fun along the way!

I'm Nate!

I'm Shea!

Located on the western Pacific Ocean coast of South America, Peru is the fourth largest country on the continent. It was the center of the great Incan civilization who later fought Spanish conquistadors who in turn ruled Peru for hundreds of years. Peru has some of the most diverse landscapes in the world from one of the world's driest deserts to the wet, species-filled Amazon rainforest; from the tall peaks of the Andes to the deepest canyon in the world: Cotahuasi.

Did you know...
- Cotahuasi Canyon is twice as deep as the Grand Canyon
- Amazon Rainforest covers an area 8 times the size of Texas
- People live on floating islands in Lake Titicaca
- The Incan Empire had 25,000 miles of roads

**In Peru's flag:**
Red = Soldiers who died for independence
White = Peace
**Coat of Arms** (not always on flag)
Vicuña = Fauna
Cincona tree = Flora
Cornucopia of gold= Mineral Wealth
Wreath = Freedom

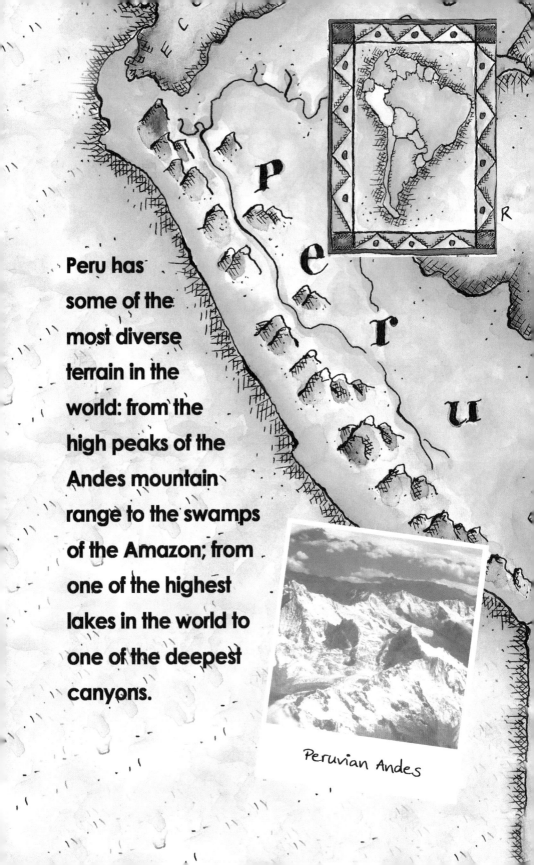

Peru has some of the most diverse terrain in the world: from the high peaks of the Andes mountain range to the swamps of the Amazon; from one of the highest lakes in the world to one of the deepest canyons.

Peruvian Andes

Early civilization

The Norte Chico civilization developed along Peru's Pacific coast around 3200BC. It is considered the oldest civilization in the Americas. In 2600BC, the large settlement at Caral built pyramid complexes; around the same time the Egyptians were building pyramids. As the Norte Chico culture declined, the Chavin, Paracas and Nazca civilizations grew. They are known for their beautiful weavings, and ceramics. Most famous are the Nazca for their geoglyphs; lines and pictures of animals made by digging a trench. No one is sure why they built them; some say to show appreciation for their gods.

Nazca Lines

This monkey is as big as a football field!

Inca Civilization

The Incan empire started in the highlands around Cusco when the ruler Manco Cápac formed the Kingdom of Cusco in the 12th century. In the 1400s, under Pachacutec, the Incan civilization began to expand. Some cultures like the Chimú and the Chanca were conquered using force; others joined the Incans peacefully. The Incans gave gifts to the people they encountered and offered them a place in their empire. If they accepted, the conquered ruler's children were brought to Cusco to learn and sometimes marry into Incan families. In the 1500s Pachacutec's grandsons, Atahualpa and Huascar started fighting for power. At the same time, the Spanish arrived and the Incan empire started to decline.

Expansion south ended at Battle of the Maule with Mapuche people

Inca Civilization

At its peak, the Inca Empire covered parts of modern day Chile, Peru, Argentina, Bolivia, Ecuador and Colombia. The main language spoken was Quechua. Big citadels and cities were connected by roads. The center of the empire, which they called Tahuantinsuyu, was Cusco. Beyond that there were four provinces stretching over 2,500 miles. Each region was connected by roads. Messengers often ran along these roads to keep people in constant contact. Parts of these roads can still be traveled on today - the most famous is the Inca Trail.

There were almost 25,000 miles of Incan roads!

Inca Gods

Viracocha is thought to be the creator god. Legend says he had three children: Inti, the sun god; Mama Killa, the goddess of the moon; and Pachamama, goddess of the earth.

Viracocha

Inca emperors are said to have descended from four brothers and sisters who were sent to earth through a cave by Inti. One brother, Manco Cápac, and his sisters placed a golden staff in Cusco, which started the empire. The people of the Incan civilization walked out of two other caves. Each mountain has its own apu or spirit god.

Incans believed their emperors were descended from sun god

Manco Cápac and Mama Ocllo

Pachacutec

Pachacutec is known as founder of the Incan Empire. Around 1435, Pachacutec won a victory against the Chanka people and became leader of the Kingdom of Cusco. Pachacutec rebuilt Cusco into a royal city

Pachacuti by Guamán Poma

in the shape of a jaguar with roads leading to regions of the empire he conquered. He built irrigation channels, terraces for farming, and huge temples like Qurikancha. His son Tupac Inca Yupanqui helped him conquer lands as far north as Ecuador.

In Quechua Pachacutec means "Changer of the world"

Cusco

Cusco was the center of the Inca Empire; its name actually means navel, or belly button, in Quechua. The ruler of each region of the empire had to live

Inca Walls, Cusco

part of the year in Cusco. In 1533, the Spanish arrived in Cusco to collect gold from Qurikancha temple for a ransom for Atahualpa. Spanish explorer Francisco Pizarro encouraged some of his people to settle there including his brothers. The three chuches on the Plaza de Armas were built by the settlers using Inca walls as their foundations.

Cristo Blanco
Cusco

Seamus' Journal

It was so fun to explore the Cusco markets and bargain with the locals.

Saksaywaman

Saksaywaman is a fort located on the northern side of Cusco. Although sections of the fort were built by the Killke people, the Incans made it much bigger in the 13th century. The fort is a great example of Incan construction with giant rocks fitted so closely that often you cannot fit a coin between them. The rocks are fitted together without any cement and the walls stand almost 20-feet high. Rooms at the fort were used to store weapons and much fighting took place between the Incans and the Spanish there.

Saksaywaman

Nathan's Journal
Subject _____
Date: / /

It's crazy how the Incans built the walls so strong without cement. And the stones were so big!

Spanish Conquistadors

After hearing about Peru's wealth from their base in Panama, in 1531, Francisco Pizarro and his men sailed south to Peru. Due to smallpox, which had spread from Central America, and Incan civil war, the Inca empire was already in decline. Pizarro captured one of the feuding Incan leaders, Atahualpa, in 1532 and was offered a wealth of gold for his return. After he received it, Atahualpa was executed. For a time, an Incan emperor of Spanish choosing ruled, but he escaped and began fighting the Spanish. After the Spanish took Cusco, the Incans

retreated to a hidden city in the hills. In 1572, the last Incan emperor was executed.

Francisco Pizarro

Pizarro meets Altahaupa

Francisco Pizarro grew up a poor, uneducated man in Spain. In 1509, he left Spain for the New World. He explored and was rewarded with a position as mayor of Panama City. There, he heard of the riches of Peru. After two failed attempts, he reached Peru in 1528 and found natives decked out in gold and silver. He returned to Spain to get permission and financing for the colonization of Peru. In 1530, along with family, friends and soldiers, he landed in South America. He captured Incan emperor Alta-huapa in 1532 and took the capital of Cusco. He left troops there, including two brothers, to settle Cusco. In 1535, he founded Lima as the capital of Peru.

Lima

Founded by Francisco Pizarro on January 18, 1535, Lima was known as Ciudad de los Reyes, or city of kings. Although Cusco was the power city of the Incan empire, Pizarro felt a coastal city was more important for the Spanish conquest. It became a center for trade and exporting mineral wealth from the continent. Along with that wealth came pirates. So, in the late 1600s, giant walls were built to protect the city. Parts of the walls can still be seen in Lima parks today. In 1821, General José de San Martín, with the help of Simón Bolívar, entered the city and signed a Declaration of Independence. After years of fighting, Peru was awarded independence from Spain in 1879. Today Lima is the second largest city in South America.

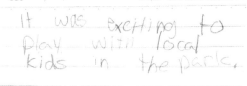

Seamus' Journal

Date / /

It was exciting to play with local kids in the park.

Language

Spanish and Quechua - the main langauge of the Incans - are the official languages in Peru. Here are some words to learn.

ENGLISH	SPANISH	PRONUNCIATION
HELLO	HOLA	OH-LAH
GOOD MORNING	BUENOS DIAS	BWEN-NOS DEE-AHS
GOOD AFTERNOON	BUENOS TARDES	BWEN-NOS TAHR-DAYS
GOOD NIGHT	BUENOS NOCHES	BWEN-NOS NO-CHESS
GOOD BYE	ADIOS	AH-DEE-OHS
WHAT IS YOUR NAME?	COMO SE LLAMA?	COH-MOH SAY YAH-MAH
MY NAME IS...	ME LLAMO ES...	MAY YAH-MOH EHS...
PLEASED TO MEET YOU	MUCHO GUSTO	MOO-CHOH GOO-STOH
PLEASE	POR FAVOR	POUR FAH-VOR
THANK YOU	GRACIAS	GRAH-SEE-AHS
HOW MUCH?	CUANTOS CUESTA?	CWAHN-TOHS CWEH-STAH?
DISCOUNT	DESCUENTO	DEHS-CWEN-TOH
WHAT IS THIS?	QUE ES ESTO?	KEH ES ES-TOH?
WHERE IS...	DONDE ESTA...	DOHN-DEH EHS-TAH
CHEERS	SALUD	SAH-LOOD
SIR/MADAM	SEÑOR/A	SEN-YOR/AH
HUSBAND/WIFE	ESPOSO/A	ES-POH-SOH/SAH
SON/DAUGHTER	HIJO/HIJA	EE-HO/EE-HA

1 - UNO - OO-NOH   4 - CUATRO - CWAH-TROH   7 - SIETE - SEE-EH-TEH
2 - DOS - DOHS   5 - CINCO - SEEN-KOH   8 - OCHO - OH-CHO
3 - TRES - TRACE   6 - SEIS - SAY-S   9 - NUEVE - NOO-EH-VEH
                                                        10 - DIEZ - DEE-ES

ENGLISH	QUECHUA	PRONUNCIATION
HOW ARE YOU?	¿ALLILLANCHU?	AY-EE-AHN-CHOO
CHEERS	¡PROSIT!	PROH-SEET
PLEASE	ALLICHU	AH-EE-CHOO

Sacred Valley

Snuggled at the base of the Andes Mountain range, the Urubamba Valley, or Sacred Valley of the Incas, was formed by the Urubamba River. The valley was at the heart of the Incan empire and has many ruins in towns like Pisac and Ollantaytambo.

Fly Over Sacred Valley
Zip lining is a cool way for kids to experience the amazing views of the Urubamba Valley. Plus, they may meet traditionally dressed locals herding their sheep!

The Incans grew much of their food here incuding many kinds of maize, or corn. They had food store houses up the mountains in cooler temperatures to keep the food fresh longer. Today, the valley is still dotted by farmers growing crops, herding sheep and making handicrafts.

El Dorado

Spanish conquistadors were drawn to Peru with tales of the wealth. Pizarro saw the amount of gold and silver when he met indigenous people in the 1500s. But, there was one tale that kept explorers coming back for more. There was a legendary city called Manoa where gold and silver were overflowing. This city was so rich that people painted themselves in gold dust and the ruler threw gold into the lake as an offering. El Dorado was marked on maps in the 16th century, but not always in the same place. Explorers searched for centuries, but to this day, no one has found the legendary lost city.

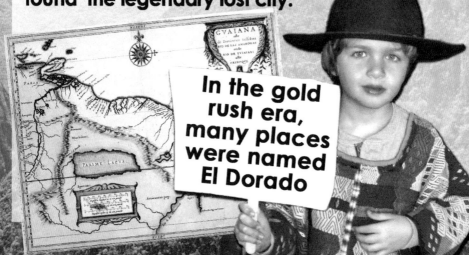

In the gold rush era, many places were named El Dorado

Hiram Bingham

Born in Hawaii in 1875, Hiram Bingham III later became a professor of South American history at Yale University. On a trip through Chile and Peru, he visited the Incan ruins at Choquequirao. Visiting it, and hearing the legends of lost cities, ignited his interst in Incan civilization. In 1911, he led his first expedition to Peru to search for the lost city of Vilcabamba, what he though to be the last hold out of the Incan Empire. On this trip, a guide led him to the lost city of Machu Picchu.

Indiana Jones character is said to be based on Bingham

Machu Picchu

Located near the Urubamba Valley, or Sacred Valley of the Incas, Machu Picchu is a citadel built high on a mountain in the 1400s. Some say it was built as a summer retreat for Incan emperor Pachacutec; however, it may have been used for sacred ceremonies as well. It was not known to outsiders until Hiram Bingham visited it in 1911. It is considered one of the New Seven Wonders of the World. The Inti Watana ritual stone found here helped predict the solstice. You can also visit the Temple of the Sun and the Temple of the Condor, but you might share the paths with llamas!

Inca Trail

The Incan road that leads to Machu Picchu is used by tourists for hiking to the site today. It's called the Inca Trail and can take four to ten days to hike. You can see where the hikers get their first look at Machu Picchu by hiking to the Sun Gate or Intipunku, which takes about an hour. The sun shines through the pilars of the gate at sunrise!

View from Sun Gate
Machu Picchu

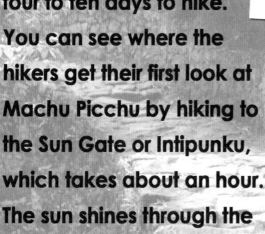

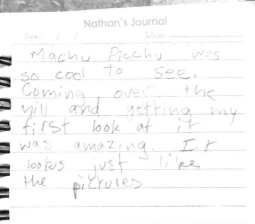

Nathan's Journal

Date: / /   Subject: _____

Machu Picchu was so cool to see. Coming over the hill and getting my first look at it was amazing. It looks just like the pictures

Pisac

Located in the Sacred Valley, Pisac is a colorful market town. On a hill above the town are Incan ruins, which were thought to guard the entrance to the Sacred Valley. Locals come to Pisac to sell fruits and vegetables and to sell traditional crafts like weaving, knit wear, wood carvings, and more to tourists. On Sundays, there is a procession through town to the local church.

Church Entrance Pisac

Pisac Market

Incan sites like Pisac and Machu Picchu are still connected by trails

Quipu

Back in Incan days, a quipu would have been used to keep track of spending at the market, or days of the month. It is a bunch of strings hanging on a main string. They used knots in the strings to keep track of things. The loops used to make each knot corresponded to a number. Quipus were used less and less after the Spanish arrived, and brought with them a written tracking system.

Quipus are similar in use to a Chinese abacus

Llamas

Llamas have long been an important part of Peru's culture. They are related to camels and can grow to six-feet tall. Llama wool, along with that of its cousins, the alpaca and the vicuña, are used to make clothes in Peru. They are also used to carry loads over long distances. They can carry as much as 100 pounds! Llamas are known for being ill-tempered and can spit as far as eight feet!

Weaving

Peruvians are known for their colorful weavings; demonstrated perfectly in jackets, chullos (hats), rugs and more. Try your hand with this simple weaving project at home! You will need a square of cardboard the size of your finished weaving, yarn in several colors in two-foot lengths, and scissors.

chullo and shawls
Cusco market

Make 1" cuts on two opposite edges of cardboard about 1/2 an inch apart. Wrap yarn around cuts opposite each-other on the cardboard and tie off. Repeat for each cut. You should end up with strands of yarn running 1/2" apart parallel to eachother on the cardboard. In opposite direction, weave yarn through these stationary pieces rotating above and below. Continue onto back of carboard, weaving above and below stationary pieces, then back onto front until length of yarn is gone. Tie off on a stationary piece and begin with new piece of yarn starting by tying it off of your last piece of yarn. Repeat until cardboard is covered. Cut stationary yarn where it loops around cardboard edges. Pull cardboard out of weaving. Tie loose ends of yarn together.

weave above and below

cut ends and pull

Music

Peru is most well known for its wind instruments, especially the siku, or panflute. Originally played by Aymara Indian women in the Lake Titicaca region, the siku is typically made from bamboo shoots or reeds cut to different lengths. Each length of bamboo produces a different note. Other popular instruments include the qina (similar to a recorder), the charango (similar to a Spanish guitar), and the bombo (large drum). The most popular Peruvian song around the world is *El Cóndor Pasa*, or *Flight of the Condor* by Daniel Alomía Robles; most famously recorded by Simon & Garfunkel.

Peruvian food

The most traditional Peruvian food is cuy, or guinea pig. But don't worry, a visit to the pet store isn't necessary to get a taste of Peru. Dishes made

Deep-fried stuffed potatoes

with potatoes and corn are also popular as well as chifa rice, ceviche and...

Lomo Saltado
- 1 lb beef tri-tip, sliced 1/4" thick
- 1 medium onion, sliced
- 1 bell pepper, sliced
- 3 tomatoes, seeded and sliced
- 1/4 cup vinegar
- 2 TBS soy sauce
- Salt and Pepper

Season sliced raw meat with salt and pepper to taste. Heat a tablespoon of olive oil in skillet. Add meat and fry for a few minutes. Remove meat. To same skillet, add onions. Cook until transparent. Add peppers and tomatoes. Cook for a few minutes. Pour in vinegar and soy sauce. Add meat back into skillet. Cook until meat is done. Traditionally, this dish is served with French fries, but it also goes with Potatoes a la Huancaina.

Ceviche
Fish cooked with lime juice

There are about 4,000 different kinds of potatoes grown in Peru

25

The Amazon River

The source of the Amazon River are smaller rivers flowing into it from Peru, Ecuador and Colombia.

Tambopata region, Amazon River

It flows 4,000 miles across South America, at some points reaching 30 miles wide. The estuary where it enters the Atlantic Ocean is 150 miles wide. It has the highest volume of water of any river in the world. Human habitation of the Amazon rainforest dates back to 8000BC. In 1542, Spanish explorer Francisco de Orellana and his men sailed all the way down the Amazon encountering many tribes along the way.

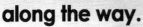

Orellana's men building ship

Amazon people

There are over 200 indigenous groups who live in the Amazon rain-forest, many of whom have had no contact with outsiders. In 2014, a plane flying over the border between Peru and Brazil spotted a tribe previously unknown to outsiders. The Asháninka are one of the largest indigenous groups living in Peru's Amazon. Other groups include the Shipibo-Conibo, Ticuna, Aguaruna, Jivaro, and the Machiguenga. They live in small communities in the rainforests.

Tambopata River
Amazon

The Jivaro tribe is known for shrinking the heads of their fallen enemies!

Tribal Life

The small communities of the Amazon traditionally live in open-air, thatch roof huts. They sleep in hammocks or on the ground. They are mostly hunter-gatherers. They hunt with bows and arrows and blow guns dipped in frog poison. Animals they eat include: fish, monkeys, rodents, and grubs. They also eat fruits and vegetables. Most tribes believe that every natural thing - earth, sky, plant, animal - has a spirit. They use plants as medicine. Shamans, or natural healers, help them with medicines and spirits.

Machiguenga hunter
Amazon

Tasting Grubs
Amazon

The people of the Amazon get around by foot and dugout canoe. Foot journeys can mean cutting away vines with a machete and crossing

Machiguenga man with painted face

Traveling by canoe Amazon

caiman-filled swamps. Some tribes do not wear clothes and pierce their faces with long spines; some wear baggy tunics they weave themselves. Many of the tribes paint their faces. This is done for many reasons including: to scare their enemies and to show you belong to a particular tribe.

Traveling by foot Amazon

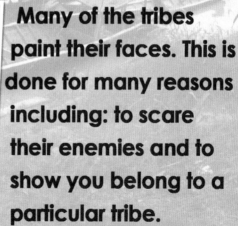

Machiguenga Tribe

The Machiguenga are a small tribe who live in the central rainforests of Peru. They grow manioc, bananas, maize, sweet potatoes and more. They also gather wild plants and herbs. In fact, they are said to know hundreds of cures for illnesses using plants in the Amazon. They fish and hunt as well. They wear cushmas, tunics, that they weave from cotton they grow.

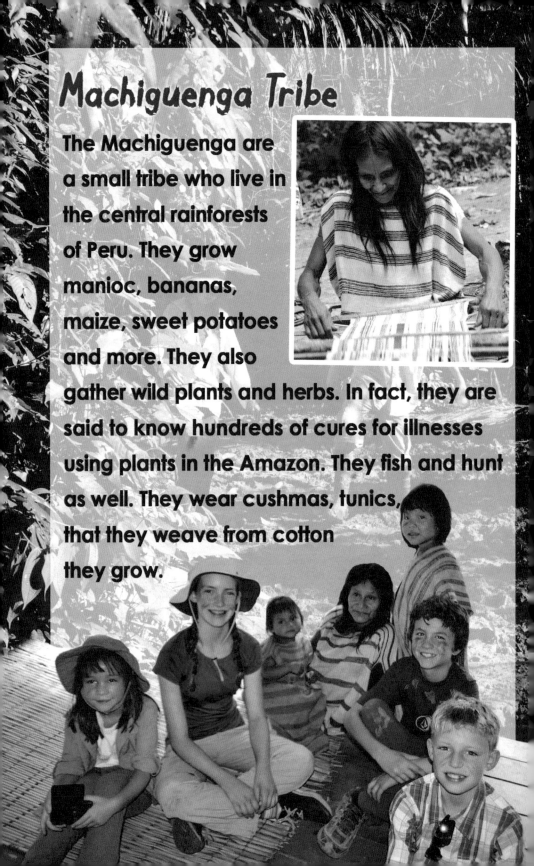

Visit to the Machiguenga

The Machiguenga family we visited lives eight days by boat from the nearest town. When we arrived, they painted our faces to welcome

us to the tribe. They showed us how to weave and spin cotton. They taught us to shoot arrows and blow darts to hunt and start fires with sticks.

Nathan's Journal

Date / / Subject

It was so cool when I got to shoot the bow and arrow although my accuracy needs work! It's amazing that they hunt that way.

Percival Harrison Fawcett

Known as Colonel Fawcett, he was born in England in 1867. In 1886, he was sent to Ceylon with the British Army. It was there that tales of treasure sparked his explorer's curiosity. In 1901 he joined the Royal Geographic Society and was sent to Brazil on their behalf just five years later to map the Amazon rainforest. Through his discoveries in the Amazon, he theorized that there was a lost city. He spent the next twenty years searching the jungles of Brazil, Peru and Bolivia for it. His son Jack joined him on a 1925 exped-ition. They were never heard from again.

Fawcett's field reports inspired Doyle's The Lost World

Amazon animals

Cool Idea:
Go on an animal hunt in your own backyard. Take pictures and see how many species you can find!

The Amazon Rainforest is home to 40,000 plant species, about 2,000 kinds of birds and mammals and almost 1,000 types of reptiles and amphibians! In addition to jaguars, river otters and pink dolphins, which are rare, here are some other big animals to look for!

Sloth

Scarlet Macaw

Caiman

Capuchin Monkey

Capybara

Amazon monkeys

The Amazon's giant trees make the perfect homes for monkeys. New species are still being discovered in remote places. Because of their prehensile tails, monkeys can swing and hang in the trees. Common types of monkeys you may see in the Amazon include tamarins, howler monkeys, spider monkeys, capuchin monkeys, squirrel monkeys and night monkeys.

Howler Monkey

Squirrel Monkey

Capuchin Monkey

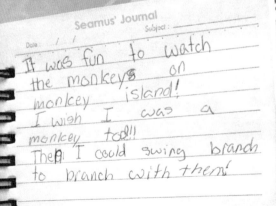

Seamus' Journal

Subject : _____

Date : / /

It was fun to watch the monkeys on monkey island!
I wish I was a monkey too!!!
Then I could swing branch to branch with them!

Creepy Crawlies

The Amazon rainforest is home to 2 1/2 million kinds of insects and over 100,000 types of invertebrates... that's a lot of creepy crawlies! Here are some you might see.

Caterpillar

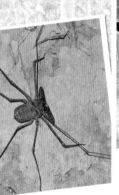

Tailess Whip Scorpion

Leaf Bug

Bullet Ant

Nathan's Journal

Date / /   Subject :

The crying beetle sounds so wierd and it pinches you and wont let go. Ouch!

Crying Beetle

Nate & Shea's Adventures provides information about destinations around the world. Learn history, culture and nature by taking a virtual trip with your guides Nate and Shea.*Nate & Shea's Adventures* can be used as a companion guide to the *Travel With Kids* video series or on their own.

Look for these other *Travel With Kids* products:

Nate & Shea's Adventures in:
Hawaii, South Africa, New York, Alaska Peru, London, Ireland, Wales, Italy, Florida

Travel With Kids (DVD):

United States:
Alaska
Florida
Hawaii: Oahu
Hawaii: Kaua'i
Hawaii: Maui & Moloka'i
Hawaii: Big Island
New York
San Diego

Caribbean:
Bahamas
Caribbean Cruise
Jamaica
Puerto Rico & Virgin Islands

Europe:
England
Greece
Ireland
Italy
London
Paris
Scotland
Wales

Latin America:
Costa Rica
Mexico: Yucatan
Mexico: Baja
Peru

Episodes covering additional destinations available on Hulu, iTunes, Amazon and more

Find out more at TravelWithKids.tv!

Enjoy learning about new places?
Get in on the fun!

Join a Travel With Kids Family Adventure Tour!

Immerse in history and culture

Discover nature

Volunteer   Reconnect time   Family time   Kid time   Adventure

TravelWithKids.tv/Tours

Made in the USA
Columbia, SC
13 January 2018